Proverbs to Live By

Wisdom From Ages Past

Proverbs to Live By

Jerome
A.
Meneely

Wisdom
From
Ages
Past

Copyright © 1998 By
NEW HORIZONS ENTERPRISES

All rights reserved.
Reproduction in whole or any parts thereof in any form
or by any media without written permission is prohibited.

First Printing: November, 1998

International Standard Book Number:

0-88290-639-9

Horizon Publishers' Catalog and Order Number:

1094

Printed and distributed in the United States of America by

Horizon
Publishers
& Distributors, Incorporated
P.O. Box 490 Bountiful, Utah 84011-0490

Proverbs to Live By

Between two evils, choose <u>neither</u>.

Between two goods, choose <u>both</u>.

Proverbs to Live By

Reputation
is precious, but
character
is priceless.

Proverbs to Live By

It's better to be
safe
than sorry.

Proverbs to Live By

Early to bed and early to rise make a man

HEALTHY,

WEALTHY,

AND WISE.

Proverbs to Live By

Count your blessings!

Proverbs to Live By

A
merry heart
is good medicine.

Proverbs to Live By

Little
strokes
fell great oaks.

Proverbs to Live By

STRAIGHT SHOOTERS
are never losers.

Proverbs to Live By

A small rudder turns a big ship.

Proverbs to Live By

Health is wealth.

Proverbs to Live By

❋❋❋

Be **busy** **as** *a* bee.

❋❋❋

Proverbs to Live By

Forgive and forget.

Proverbs to Live By

Practice makes PERFECT.

Proverbs to Live By

The early bird gets the worm.

Proverbs to Live By

WASTE NOT, WANT NOT.

Proverbs to Live By

A stitch in time
saves nine.

Proverbs to Live By

PRIDE
goeth before a
fall

Proverbs to Live By

You are
what you
eat.

Proverbs to Live By

If you **fail** to prepare, prepare to **fail**.

Proverbs to Live By

Oh what tangled webs we weave when we practice to deceive.

Proverbs to Live By

Be like a good watch:
full of good works,
busy hands,
and well run.

Proverbs to Live By

The sign
on the door of opportunity says,

> *Push.*

Proverbs to Live By

*

*To
get to
the top,
start at the*
bottom.

Proverbs to Live By

We have met
the enemy
and he is us.

We have met
the enemy
and he is us.

Proverbs to Live By

Counting time
is less important than
making time count.

Proverbs to Live By

It's better to *understand*
a little
than to *misunderstand*
a lot.

Proverbs to Live By

Character is easier to keep than to recover.

Proverbs to Live By

You can't judge a book by it's cover.

Proverbs to Live By

The wheat gets separated from the chaff.

Proverbs to Live By

Fools rush in

where angels fear to tread.

Proverbs to Live By

Let bygones be bygones.

Proverbs to Live By

mountain
every
Climb

Proverbs to Live By

Where there's a *will* there's a way.
∧

Proverbs to Live By

Circumstances won't change you;

they reveal you.

Proverbs to Live By

You need the **right tools** to do the job **right**.

Proverbs to Live By

Be it ever so humble, there's no place like home.

Proverbs to Live By

YOU CAN ATTRACT
MORE FLIES WITH
HONEY
THAN YOU CAN WITH
VINEGAR.

Proverbs to Live By

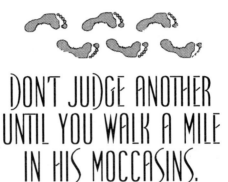

DON'T JUDGE ANOTHER UNTIL YOU WALK A MILE IN HIS MOCCASINS.

Proverbs to Live By

Worry is waste.

Proverbs to Live By

You REAP *what you* SOW.

44

Proverbs to Live By

It is more blessed to
Give
than to receive.

Proverbs to Live By

. . . Patience . . . . is a virtue.

Proverbs to Live By

Idle hands

⧗ ⧗ ⧗ ⧗ ⧗ ⧗

are the devil's workshop.

Proverbs to Live By

All that glitters

is not gold.

Proverbs to Live By

EMPTY BARRELS
make the most noise.

Proverbs to Live By

Sometimes you can't see the forest for the trees.

Proverbs to Live By

There's **no** honor among thieves.

Proverbs to Live By

The road to ruin is wide and well traveled.

Proverbs to Live By

Put your best foot forward.

Proverbs to Live By

Don't burn your
BRIDGES
behind you.

Proverbs to Live By

It's the thought that counts.

Proverbs to Live By

Burn the midnight oil.

Proverbs to Live By

A spoonful of
sugar
makes the medicine go down.

Proverbs to Live By

Seek

and ye shall find.

Proverbs to Live By

The grass is always greener on the other side.

Proverbs to Live By

Don't
Rain on my **parade**.

Proverbs to Live By

TWO WRONGS DON'T MAKE A RIGHT.

Proverbs to Live By

Your *reach*

should always exceed

your grasp

Proverbs to Live By

The
spirit is willing,
but the flesh is weak.

Proverbs to Live By

A hasty word is like a boomerang.

Proverbs to Live By

As the twig is bent, so the tree grows.

Proverbs to Live By

A tiny flame lights *a big blaze.*

Proverbs to Live By

If you lie down with dogs, you may get up with

Proverbs to Live By

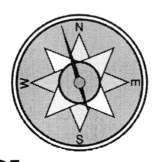

Character
is the compass of life.

Proverbs to Live By

IT'S AN ILL WIND THAT BLOWS NO GOOD.

Proverbs to Live By

Wealth *is a way of looking at* LIFE.

Proverbs to Live By

Time and tide
wait
for
no one.

Proverbs to Live By

To walk with the wise is wise. Be wise!

Proverbs to Live By

What goes up must come down.

Proverbs to Live By

Don't put off till tomorrow WHAT YOU CAN DO TODAY.

Proverbs to Live By

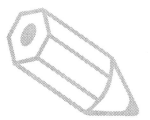

A WORD TO THE <u>WISE</u> IS SUFFICIENT.

Proverbs to Live By

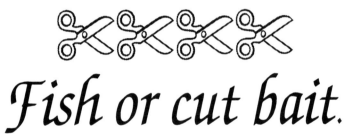

Fish or cut bait.

Proverbs to Live By

What a difference
a **day**
makes.

Proverbs to Live By

A FOOL AND HIS MONEY ARE SOON PARTED.

Proverbs to Live By

ROME
WASN'T BUILT IN A DAY

Proverbs to Live By

THE WAY OF THE
TRANSGRESSOR
IS hard.

Proverbs to Live By

Rich or poor, you can always afford to be *Nice.*

Proverbs to Live By

You can be better or bitter.

Proverbs to Live By

If you want to kill time,
try WORKING it to death.

Proverbs to Live By

ABSOLUTE POWER CORRUPTS ABSOLUTELY.

Proverbs to Live By

Give a man a fish
and he'll eat for a day;
teach him **how** to fish
and he'll eat for a lifetime.

Proverbs to Live By

Without
vision
the people perish.

Proverbs to Live By

If you dance, you have to pay the piper.

Proverbs to Live By

DO WHAT IS RIGHT,
let the **consequence** follow.

Proverbs to Live By

United we stand, divided we fall.

Proverbs to Live By

YOU MUST KNOW
THE BITTER
to appreciate
the **sweet**.

Proverbs to Live By

An ounce of
prevention
is worth a pound of
cure.

Proverbs to Live By

If you don't control your mind, it will control you.

Proverbs to Live By

Meditation
is the language of the soul.

Proverbs to Live By

GENIUS
is but perseverance
in disguise.

Proverbs to Live By

Wisdom IS KNOWING
WHAT TO DO NEXT;
Virtue IS DOING IT.

Proverbs to Live By

THE
GREATEST HOMAGE
WE CAN PAY TO

Truth

IS TO USE IT.

Proverbs to Live By

Don't let **yesterday** **erode** **today** and steal **tomorrow.**

Proverbs to Live By

You can't weigh
a good **deed**,
a kind **word**,
or a loving **heart**.

Proverbs to Live By

A rotten apple spoils the barrel.

Proverbs to Live By

Politeness
is to human nature
as warmth is
to wax.

Proverbs to Live By

Too
soon
old , too
late
smart.

Proverbs to Live By

Drive Carefully!

Motorists can be recalled by their Maker.

Proverbs to Live By

No sadder words
of voice or pen
than these four words,
"IT MIGHT
HAVE BEEN."

Proverbs to Live By

Kindness
covers everything with beauty.

Proverbs to Live By

THERE'S NO TIME LIKE THE PRESENT.

Proverbs to Live By

Only you can
damage your character.

Proverbs to Live By

When was the last time
you told your mother
you love her?
<u>Hurry</u>, it may be your last chance.

Proverbs to Live By

What goes around,
comes around.

Proverbs to Live By

Here today,
gone tomorrow.

Proverbs to Live By

Never play with
fire.

Proverbs to Live By

If it isn't **ONE** thing, it's **another**.

Proverbs to Live By

To err is human, to forgive, *Divine*

Proverbs to Live By

Love
is the key
that opens the door to
Happiness.

Proverbs to Live By

Cleanliness
is next to
Godliness.

Proverbs to Live By

A happy home

is priceless.

Proverbs to Live By

*Choice,
not chance,
determines destiny.*

Proverbs to Live By

Education is not **received**.
It is **achieved**.

Proverbs to Live By

Happiness

is a by-product of achievement.

Proverbs to Live By

Say nothing often.

Proverbs to Live By

The greatest remedy for **anger** is

. . . **delay**.

Proverbs to Live By

An ounce of **facts** is worth a ton of arguments.

arguments arguments

Proverbs to Live By

Faith with works is a

force.

Faith <u>without</u> works is a

farce.

Proverbs to Live By

No man has a **RIGHT**
to do as he **PLEASES**,
except when he **PLEASES**
to do **RIGHT**.

Proverbs to Live By

Happiness

is in the heart,

not in the circumstances.

Proverbs to Live By

Few burdens are *heavy* when EVERYBODY LIFTS.

Proverbs to Live By

The smallest
⚜⚜⚜ **good deed** ⚜⚜⚜
is better than the grandest

intention.

Index

Accuracy - 39
Angels - 34
Anger - 120
Another - 111
Appreciation - 9
Arguments - 121
Around - 108
Bait - 76
Barrels - 49
Beauty - 104
Bitter - 82, 90
Blaze - 66
Blessings - 9, 45
Boomerang - 64
Book - 32
Bottom - 27
Bridges - 54
Burdens - 125

Burn - 54, 56
Busy - 15
Bygones - 35
Chaff - 33
Character - 6, 31, 68, 106
Choosing - 5, 116
Circumstances - 38, 124
Cleanliness - 114
Climb - 36
Compass - 68
Consequences - 44, 88
Control - 92
Corruption - 84
Cure - 91
Dance - 87

Day - 77, 79
Deception - 24
Destiny - 116
Determination - 11, 13, 26, 27, 36, 37
Devil - 47
Divided - 89
Divine - 112
Dogs - 67
Down - 73
Driving - 102
Early - 18
Eating - 22
Education - 117
Enemy - 28
Error - 112
Evils - 5

Fail - 23
Fairness - 61
Faith - 122
Fall - 21
Fire - 110
Fish - 76, 85
Flame - 66
Fleas - 67
Fools - 34, 78
Foot - 53
Forest - 50
Forgiveness - 16, 112
Forward - 53
Genius - 94
Giving - 45
Glitters - 48
Gold - 48

Grass - 59
Grasp - 62
Greener - 59
Growth - 65, 79
Happiness - 10, 115, 113, 118, 124
Hasty - 64
Health - 8, 14, 18
Homage - 96
Home - 40, 115
Honesty - 12
Honey - 41
Honor - 51
Humble - 40
Idleness - 47
Intention - 126
Judgment - 32, 42

Index

Kindness - 104
Language - 93
Life - 70
Losers - 12
Love - 113, 107, 98
Medicine - 10, 57
Meditation - 93
Merry - 10
Midnight - 56
Might - 103
Moccasins - 42
Money - 78
Mothers - 107
Nice - 81
Noise - 49
One - 111
Parade - 60
Patience - 46
Perfect - 17

Perish - 86
Perseverance - 94
Piper - 87
Politeness - 100
Practice - 17
Prepare - 23
Present - 105
Prevention - 91
Pride - 21
Poor - 81
Poverty - 81
Power - 84
Push - 26
Rain - 60
Reach - 62
Reap - 44
Regret - 103
Reputation - 6
Reveal - 38
Rich - 81

Right - 123
Rome - 79
Rotten - 99
Rudder - 13
Ruin - 52
Safety - 7
Seek - 58
Service - 25
Ship - 13
Sign - 26
Silence - 119
Smart - 101
Sorry - 7
Sow - 44
Stitch - 20
Strokes - 11
Sugar - 57
Sweet - 90
Teaching - 85
Thieves - 51

Thought - 55
Time - 29, 71, 83, 105
Today - 74, 109, 97
Tomorrow - 74, 109, 97
Tools - 39
Transgressor - 80
Trees - 50
Truth - 96
Twig - 65
Understanding - 30
Unity - 89
Up - 73
Vinegar - 41
Virtue - 95
Vision - 86
Warmth - 100

Waste - 19, 43
Watch - 25
Weak - 63
Wealth - 8, 14, 60
Webs - 24
Weigh - 98
Wheat - 33
Will - 37
Willing - 63
Wind - 69
Wisdom - 8, 9, 72, 75, 95
Word - 75
Working - 83
Worm - 18
Worry - 4
Wrongs - 61
Yesterday - 97

128